Eff

This book belongs to

Peter + Jenny

Other books by the author:

How to Have Victory Over Sin
Discovering Your Destiny
Intimacy with God

The Father Heart of God
Father Make Us One
Living on the Devil's Doorstep
Just Off Chicken Street
Nine Worlds to Win

Effective Evangelism

A guide to friendship evangelism

Floyd McClung, Jr.
with Geoff and Janet Benge

Marshall Pickering

Marshall Morgan and Scott
Marshall Pickering
3 Beggarwood Lane, Basingstoke, Hants RG23 7LP, UK

First published in 1988 by Marshall Morgan and Scott
Publications Ltd
Part of the Marshall Pickering Holdings Group
A subsidiary of the Zondervan Corporation

ISBN: 0 551 01725 2

Text Set in Plantin by Brian Robinson, Buckingham
Printed in Great Britain by Cox and Wyman, Reading

Contents

Acknowledgement

I wish to express my indebtedness and appreciation to Geoff and Janet Benge who helped write this booklet. Their names should really be on the cover.
Geoff and Janet have been faithful friends and wonderful co-authors. Many of the ideas shared here came through the stimulation of conversations with them in meeting places as varied as Bozeman, Montana and Amsterdam, Holland. Thank you Geoff and Janet, for your friendship and for standing with me through the development of this booklet. I am very grateful.

Floyd McClung
Amsterdam, Holland

Effective Evangelism

There are a great number of well-meaning Christians who think evangelism is accomplished with tracts and words alone. They see evangelism as an isolated activity, it is something you 'do' until it is 'done' and then you find another person to 'do' it too.

In the pages of this small book I pray you will begin to see the whole picture of evangelism. It is wider than handing out tracts or preaching on the streets; even though it includes that. It involves our entire life and how we choose to live it before others.

Evangelism is also something we do when we actively share our faith. It involves drama and music, and meetings and conversation. It means standing for justice, and giving mercy, being thoughtful to a friend in need, and being available when someone is down. It is praying for the sick and confronting evil when others are oppressed. This booklet is intended to give practical help in sharing our faith, as well as dispel common misconceptions about leading men to Christ. It is my conviction that we lead people to Christ by inviting them to follow our very lives, day in and day out. This is everyday evangelism . . .

Chapter One

Follow me as I follow Christ

Joe has a great relationship with his five-year-old son, Nick. It's the sort of relationship that makes you smile when you see them together, heads bent over exploring an ant-hill they've come upon, or running and laughing flying a home-made kite in a field. I once commented to Joe about the fact that I admired the way he took so much time out from his already crowded schedule to spend time with his son. His response was interesting. He told me he wanted Nick to grow up and embrace his ideals – to love serving the Lord and care for the world around him. Joe felt that for Nick to enter into his world, he first had to enter into his son's world, and *so he worked at becoming his son's best friend*. Joe built bridges into Nick's life through playing games with him, talking and listening and caring.

Joe's desire to reach out to his son is very much like God's desire to be our friend. Paul tells us that Jesus '. . . emptied himself, taking the form of a bond-servant, and being made in the likeness of men' (Philippians 2:7). Jesus entered our world to show us the Father. He came as a friend to those who needed Him.

In John's gospel Jesus tells us, 'as the Father sent Me, I also send you'(John 20:21). Jesus makes it clear in this passage that He not only wants us to reach out to others, but to do it as He would if He were in our place. In the same manner He was sent to us, He has authorized us to go to others. If we are to go to others in the same manner Christ was sent to us, it raises the obvious question – in what manner was He sent to us?

Firstly, Jesus gave up His rights in order to come to us. He left His home, gave up fellowship with His Father, and laid aside every divine right He had. We live in a 'rights'-oriented world. Everyone is conscious of what is rightfully theirs, and normally they demand it as well. The person who gives up his rights, particularly in order to build friendships and solve conflicts with others, has the power of unselfish love on his side. This way of living is attractive because of its unselfishness.

Secondly, He was a servant. 'Do you know what I have done for you? You call me teacher and Lord, and you are right for so I am. If I then, the Lord and the teacher, washed your feet, you also ought to wash one another's feet' (John 13:12 – 14). In the Western world we can become so familiar with the Gospel that we lose sight of the astounding paradoxes in it. The Son of God came into our world to be a servant! In today's world where authority denotes rank, it's hard to imagine the head of a major corporation assigning his capable son to scrub the office floors for thirty-three years. If there's one person in the universe who deserves to be served it is Jesus, the Son of the Creator God, yet He came not to be served, but to serve.

Thirdly, Jesus came as a friend. He was available to people in all manner of situations. He encouraged people, He listened to them. He was honest, forgiving, and accepting. He had principles, so He was someone they easily respected. In short, He was a genuine friend. He was the kind of person people felt they could share their problems with and He would understand.

Finally, Jesus was obedient. 'My food is to do the will of Him who sent Me, and to accomplish His work' (John

4:34). Jesus' obedience stood strong, even when tested to its limits in the garden of Gethsemane as He anguished over his impending death on the cross. This commitment to truth gave Jesus genuine spiritual authority. He came to do the works of His Father (John 12:49). Because of His love for truth, people were attracted to Him.

So, Jesus came to earth as a servant; He had authority, gave up His rights, and was obedient to His Father, even when that meant an excruciating death. In the same way He sends us to others. It is not enough to just have zeal and enthusiasm. If we are to be effective in evangelism we must go about it in the same manner as Jesus did.

We must earn the right to speak into the lives of others. God could have written the instructions for salvation in the sky. Instead, He chose the most intimate and personal of ways – He sent His Son. Jesus lived His life openly and in full view of others. He invited the disciples to learn both from what He said, and from how He lived His life. We, too, must do the same if we are to be credible witnesses. Words lack the power to bring conviction and change if they are not reflected in the life of the person speaking.

Several years ago some workers from Youth with a Mission went to establish a ministry among Vietnamese refugees who were being held in a camp in Hong Kong. When they first asked for permission to enter the camp it was denied, but they persisted, and were eventually allowed to enter the camp. The camp supervisor, however, suspected them to be just another group of 'do-gooders' who would not last, forbade them to do anything 'evangelistic'. Instead, they were assigned to work at restoring a blocked and overflowing toilet system. For days the team laboured knee deep in squalid waste. They scrubbed, cleaned and mended broken and blocked pipes until the toilet system was once again fully operational.

When they reported to the supervisor for their next task he confided that he'd never expected them to complete the first one. He was so impressed with their attitude and willingness to work that he opened the camp to them to run evangelistic programmes among the Vietnamese people. The team soon found that the Vietnamese people, who had watched keenly as they restored the broken toilet system, had been touched by what they saw. They were ready and eager to listen to the Gospel message that the team had to share with them.

Chapter Two

Will I Witness Today?

Witnessing cannot be turned off and on like a machine – it is not just an act of the will. Witnessing is not just something we do, it is who we are. Our life and the way we live it daily, bears witness to what we truly believe. Everything we choose to do, or not to do, our attitudes, the way we treat others, our words, all have an impact on someone, and we cannot go through a day or week without our life influencing somebody. The question is not *will* we witness, but *how* will we witness.

By perceiving witnessing to be merely going out on the streets on a Friday night, or handing out tracts, we miss the wider implication of our life – every minute of every day being a witness.

Some years ago in the north-western United States, a prominent minister was visiting outlying parishes under his pastoral control. In one town he stayed at the local hotel for several days and as he was checking out the desk clerk, assuming him to be a travelling salesman, asked what he was selling. 'What do you think I sell?' the minister replied. The clerk was quick to gues, 'Oh, I bet you're a whisky salesman'. The minister did not reply and walked away saddened, wondering what it was in his behaviour had led the clerk to make such a conclusion. Likewise, people constantly draw conclusions about us based solely on how they see us live and act.

Integrity in witnessing occurs when our words line up with the way we live our life. Paul, writing to the church at Corinth, says, 'For the kingdom of God does not consist in words, but in power' (1 Corinthians 4:20). Powerful evangelism is evangelism that has integrity, that flows from a life committed to being a faithful witness.

Many of us have heard or read the testimonies of people who said the way a certain person reacted to a situation made them rethink their opinion of Christianity. They were so impressed by the quality of life they saw in others that they began reaching out for what they saw. What do people think of us when we are under stress? Are we the type of witness people admire? Even the 'little things' in our lives can have a significant impact on others.

In Amsterdam, as in all big cities, we spend a lot of time waiting in lines in the shops, and department stores we frequent. Enetha, one of our co-workers, tries to always ask God for an extra amount of patience and friendliness when she has to wait. Recently she found herself the last in line to be served at a souvenir shop. Some of those ahead of her were becoming irritable and restless, so when Enetha's turn came to be served she purposely reacted in a different manner from those ahead of her. She commented on how nice the sales girl looked and asked her name. She found out it was Marie, and asked her if it was a family name. Marie explained how her parents had known a wonderful Christian woman named Marie, and she had been named after her. Marie went on to tell Enetha she only attended church twice a year and had been wondering lately if that was all there was to being a Christian! Their conversation proved so fruitful that they agreed to meet later and continue it. At their next meeting Marie confided that she had no idea why she mentioned about going to church, but had been so impressed by the way Enetha acted toward her that she just found herself pouring out her heart.

Jesus pointed out to the Pharisees that, 'the mouth speaks out of that which fills the heart' (Matthew 12:34b). If our hearts are not filled with love for God it will soon show in our words. We cannot lead a person any closer to Jesus than we are ourselves, or show them spiritual truth unless it is first a firm reality in our life. To attempt to do this is the difference between effective evangelism and hypocrisy.

Chapter Three

Three Principles of Evangelism

The gospels record Jesus ministering in a variety of situations. He stood on the side of a mountain and taught the multitudes about the Kingdom of God. He spoke with a Samaritan woman as she drew water from a well. He fed five thousand people, and ate privately at the home of Zaccheus, the tax collector. Whether it was a few people or many, he was always comfortable and able to minister with power and effectiveness. He took the time to identify with his audience. He listened to them, found out their needs, and then ministered to those needs. To be effective evangelists we must follow his pattern.

Identification

Occasionally people say to me, 'I could never do what you are doing – I could never live in the inner-city, talk to drug addicts, or a prostitute or an alcoholic.' I respond by telling people that my testimony is that I am the guy who tried to smoke half a cigarette when I was a lad and it made me sick! Identification with non-Christians does not depend on what we have been through in the past, but on what the Holy Spirit does in our heart now.

The computer programmer who has rejected Christ is

as much a sinner as a prostitute, or thief, or murderer. We are all sinners and in need of the love and forgiveness of God. It does not matter whether a person is drowning five feet from the side of a swimming pool, or five miles out to sea, the fact is they are drowning and are in need of rescue.

Jesus provides for us some examples of what it means to identify with others. Jewish culture in his day was very structured; lepers were outcasts; women were subservient; doctrinal differences created permanent rifts. The Samaritans, for example, had different views on where God should be worshipped and had intermarried with the Assyrians, and so had been separated completely from the mainstream of Jewish life and culture. Against this background Jesus came and touched the lepers, spoke to and respected women, walked through Samaria and talked to its inhabitants, and taught all who would listen. He did not condemn the people He ministered to, but instead showed them the utmost respect. He put himself in their place, felt what they felt, laughed when they laughed, and cried when they cried. In so doing He identified with them and their needs.

Jesus was without sin. Yet, when confronted with people who had committed sin, He did not respond in any condescending or judgmental manner. He never condoned sin, but, while hating the sin, He loved the person and never lost sight of all God could do in their life. Having been forgiven by God, we have all the more reason to idenfity with those we are reaching out to. Identification in evangelism means that, without compromise, we enter into the life and feelings of those to whom we are witnessing.

To be effective in evangelism we must identify with the non-Christians around us. When we respond to a person out of genuine love and respect the walls they have built around their life begin to crumble.

Listening

All too often in our eagerness to talk to people about the Gospel we fail to take the time to listen to their concerns. We start conversations in which we don't really want to hear the other person's point of view, but are just waiting for a lull in the conversation so we can pounce in with our 'prepackaged' Gospel presentation.

We need to listen intelligently to other people. Ask questions and find out what their views are. Try to draw a person's thoughts out and then rephrase what they have said to be sure we understand them. When a person senses we are interested in what they are saying, they are likely to open up further. Effective listening has an impact upon those we talk to. Besides, we have a lot to learn from others!

Body language is also important to being a good listener. If our mouth is saying one thing and our body another, the person we are speaking to will be confused. Watch tendencies to fidget, to look elsewhere, and to do other distracting things which unconsciously convey a lack of interest in what the person is saying. Learn to look a person straight in the eyes. Nothing is more off putting than a person who peers over your shoulder when you talk to them.

It is also good to remember a person's name. This is not always easy, but asking their name and then using it several times in the first few minutes of conversation is one way to help lodge it in your mind. If you think you will see the person again, write down their name and memorize it.

The suggestions above come down to showing respect for the person we are witnessing to. When people talk to us they tell us things that matter to them, and if, in our opinion, their views are strange, illogical, weird, or unreasonable, we must still show respect. People have a right to their views, and we should be honoured that they took the time to share them with us.

Responding in Love and Wisdom

Though a person's separation from God is their most obvious need to us as Christians, it is not necessarily that which must be addressed first. Other needs, such as friendship and acceptance, a place to stay, food to eat, dignity and self esteem, are often the felt needs of the person you want to befriend. Taking care of those needs will open a door of friendship through which we can minister to their needs to know Christ as Saviour.

There are three basic inherited human needs that are common to us all. These needs must be recognized and respected in all human relationships. Evangelism that ignores these needs can end up being very impersonal in nature.

All people have a need to belong, and to be wanted. God created us as social beings. We were created for friendship and relationship. No programme or method of evangelism can meet this need. There is simply no replacement for genuine friendship and acceptance.

Then there is the need for significance and importance. We all want and appreciate respect and dignity. We are created in God's image, therefore we have value. Our choices have meaning, even when they are the wrong choices. When we approach people it should be with the upmost respect for their opinions, ideas, and choices. We give affirmation to others and thus help affirm their worth and value before God when we treat them in this manner.

The third human need requires security and safety. When this need is not met, the result is fear – one of the most powerful human emotions. By being sensitive to people, by loving them and being kind, we create room for security in the relationship. Love drives away fear, but a lack of love creates insecurity and uncertainty, which is *never* conducive to evangelism.

Larry and Jan moved into a new apartment building about a year and a half ago. Soon they were busy introducing themselves to their new neighbours. Over time their friendly, outgoing attitude and their willingness to listen to their neighbours had an effect on the residents of the apartment building, and so, about nine months later, they were not too surprised when a couple from a neighbouring apartment came to visit unexpectedly. With tears in their eyes they explained how the Jehovah's Witnesses had come to their door only wanting them to change their religion. On the other hand, Larry and Jan had been different. They had cared for them, respected them, listened, and understood what they were feeling. As a result, this couple wanted to know more about Larry and Jan's faith in God. The four of them now have a regular Bible study together.

Jan and Larry learned the secret of reaching a person at their point of 'felt need'.

Chapter Four

Talking About the Truth

We may not always have the luxury of time and so must learn to balance the need to earn the right to speak about Christ, and the Holy Spirit leading us in a situation where we should speak about eternal truths. On an aeroplane, for example, there is only limited time to speak with others. In these situations we must follow the Spirit's leading. Perhaps he wants us to jump right into the conversation and ask about their interests in spiritual matters. If their response is negative, that's okay. If they do not want to talk, do not force the issue. In those situations, it is important for us to learn to obey God's promptings. It is our responsibility to obey God, but not to force a conversation.

Other times we may not want to open a religious conversation at all, but instead just talk to the person about their interests in life. Regardless of how we are led, we must be sensitive to the person. Don't force situations. If the person is interested great. If not, pray for them.

As Christians we often have a narrow field of interests which may leave us at a disadvantage. Not only does it confirm to the non-Christian's mind that Christians are boring and rather ignorant of the world around them, but it also provides us with little common ground. It is important for Christians to keep abreast of what is happening in the world around them. We should read as widely as possible, taking interest in the world around us. In broadening our horizons this way we provide ourselves with information that will help us to more easily enter into conversation.

Recently I flew to South Africa. Across the aisle from me on the plane sat a young lady and we began a conversation. We started by talking about very general things, the weather, how calm the flight was, and other things of that nature. As the conversation developed she told me she worked with KLM and had been in Amsterdam for a training progamme. I asked about her work and how she enjoyed it, all the while praying the Lord would lead in our conversation.

Eventually she asked me what I did and calmly I responded, 'I work with prostitutes in Amsterdam.' She gave me a surprised look and I went on to tell her that we – myself, my wife and our two young children – live in the red light district of the city. I described to her, in fairly sociological terms at first, what we were doing. As we continued I began to weave the Gospel more and more into the conversation. 'The reason we're involved is because those girls have value, regardless of what they've done. I believe every person has great value and worth to God.'

She told me she was a Catholic and prayed to Mary. It seemed her way of saying, 'you believe your way and I will believe mine'. I noticed she watched me very intently to see what my reaction was.

After the lapse of some time she looked over and asked me what I thought about praying to Mary. I thought for a moment and felt the Spirit give me direction. 'I have a lot of Catholic friends. Some of them pray to Mary because they don't feel they're worthy enough to pray to Jesus'. I became aware of the Holy Spirit's presence in my conversation at that moment. I explained how, for much of my Christian life, I'd lived under a list of rules and had not experienced a relationship with Jesus based on His love for me. One day, as my college professor taught on Galatians, it suddenly hit me – God loves me. I could come to him and ask His forgiveness based on His love for me. 'That is the most wonderful thing that ever happened to me,' I told her.

Big tears rolled down her cheeks, 'I've never heard anything like that before. It's so beautiful.' At that moment the Holy Spirit was giving her understanding of God's love for her. My goal was not to force something on her that she did not want but, in the context of mutual respect for our beliefs, and respect for each other in spite of serious disagreements over our beliefs, to share my understanding of the Gospel. I had the satisfaction of knowing she left the plane with a clear and deep understanding of God's love for her.

I like to think witnessing is a little like fishing. You bait the hook and throw it into the water. If there's a nibble you draw it in a little. It takes patience. You wait, draw the line in a little again, and wait for the fish to renew its interest. When you feel the fish has a firm hold of the bait and hook you begin reeling it in. In witnessing we follow the same procedure. Most Christians take the rod and beat people over the head, and then they wonder why people don't respond to them! We shouldn't give a 20-point sermon on justification by faith and then make a quick exit. Instead, we should whet a person's curiosity by sharing things that are precious to us in the hope that they will want to know more.

Jesus was a master of this. He told parables that whetted people's interest. They would think about what He had said and ask Him for more clarification. From there He would go on and share the deeper truths He wanted to communicate. John chronicled Jesus' conversation with a Samaritan woman drawing water from a well. He used 'living water' as a way of getting her attention. It caught the woman's curiosity and by the end of their conversation her life was touched and changed forever (John 4:4–44).

Evangelism is not just talking. Talking plays an important part in evangelism but, ultimately, it is the motive behind what we say and the attitude in which we speak, rather than the actual words we use that makes the greatest impact. Genuineness and honesty, not eloquence, will win the hearts of men and women. People want to see that we really care for and understand them. When they see that we do they will open up to the message we have to share with them It may take time, but it is time well spent. In the end, they don't care how much we know until they know how much we care.

Chapter Five

Patience in Evangelism

Patience and perseverance are necessities for friendship evangelism. In an instant world it's easy to look for instant success in evangelism. However, there are no short cuts. No matter how good our tracts may be, or how thorough our witnessing programme is, there are no substitutes for taking time to develop relationships with the people we are seeking to lead to the Lord. There may be times when we spend weeks, months, even years, just praying for a person's salvation before we ever have the opportunity to witness to them.

Over the past five years, Sally and I have had our hair cut at a small salon located in one of Amsterdam's tourist hotels. The salon is not run by Christians, the owner is gay and some of the customers are prostitutes. However, we feel God wants us to go there and be real friends with the people who work there.

Marion, the young lady who cuts our hair, was very defensive when we tried to talk to her about the Lord, and would refuse to talk at length about anything. I really wanted to share with her, and sometimes got discouraged at her response. At times I would pray all the way to the salon and while my hair was being cut, and still nothing happened. I would feel totally frustrated. However, when I was tempted to give up I always heard the Lord saying, 'Be patient, I'm going to touch her heart'.

Several months ago a turning point came in an unusal way. A man came to the salon claiming to be a Christian. He asked one of the girls out and afterwards tried to seduce her. Everyone at the salon was indignant about the incident. What had upset them most was that the man had said he was a Christian. The next time Sally went to the salon Marion told her the story and commented, 'That man was not a Christian like Floyd. I trust Floyd. I know Floyd – he would never do a thing like that.'

Not long afterwards I went to have my hair cut. I said to Marion, 'Thank you for what you said to Sally. I'm glad you trust me. Sally and I both love you and are very committed to you.' There was a breakthrough that day in our friendship. We are able to be open and honest with each other, and many times when I go to the salon she wants to talk about Christian things. She is not a Christian yet, but is softening toward it each time we talk.

It took five years of patience and perseverance with Marion before the seeds of the Gospel began to take root in her heart. At times it was frustrating and seemed pointless, but now those years of perseverance, of walking across town to the salon while I prayed fervently, are reaping results.

Friendship evangelism is not for the impatient or intolerant.

Chapter Six

A Checklist of Attitudes

Several years ago Janet, a worker with Youth with a Mission, was witnessing on Waikiki beach in Hawaii. She struck up a conversation with a middle-aged man, and when it became apparent to him she was a Christian he pulled a Bible from his shirt pocket. Janet was somewhat taken aback when he began flipping from one underlined passage to another which 'proved' God was a vengeful and hateful God. Every time she said something he would find another scripture to confirm his distorted view of God until it became impossible to continue the conversation. As it transpired, this man had been hurt by the attitudes of Christians who had witnessed to him in the past. So, he had taken the trouble to study the Bible and carry it with him so he could ward off anyone else who tried to talk to him about the Lord.

Humility not Humiliation

There are those Christians determined to bully others into agreeing with them regardless of the cost to human relationships. They do not understand that we are not called to dominate and conquer people. We are to be witnesses, not warriors, in the cause of evangelism. We are not out to conquer by sheer force of will and words those to whom we witness.

Most of us have had a person from a cult come to our door and attempt to convince us they're right and we're wrong. It is an experience few of us enjoy! They may be sincere, yes, but treat us more like objects than people. Their main aim seems to be getting through their pre-learned presentation.

While we may also feel uncomfortable and frustrated by this sort of approach ourselves, we often use it on non-Christians. I am not saying we shouldn't go door-to-door – we should! We should also go out on the streets, to the park, shopping malls and any other place where we can break into people's complacent lifestyles. The key, however, is to love people, not manipulate them. Let them sense our love and concern, challenging their minds, present the Gospel in creative ways – ways that will cause them to think, but in the end respect their right and ability to make their own choice about what we share.

I believe it is important to find common ground with the person we're witnessing to. It is much easier to work from some commonly held interest or belief than it is to attack a person's beliefs, which only serves to put them on the defensive. Don't outrightly ask the person if they are a Christian. If they answer yes, but seem to have little grasp of what being a Christian really is, we end up trying to catch inconsistencies in their beliefs so we can show them they are not really a believer after all – and that is a negative way to witness.

Paul was the master at finding common ground. When addressing the philosophers at the Aeropagus he did not say, 'Listen you misguided philosophers. Your God is dead. You're wasting your time praying to idols. I have the right religion, so, be quiet and I will tell you about the true, loving, and gracious God.' Instead, he started out on common ground. 'Men of Athens, I observe that you are very religious in all respects. For, while I was passing through and examining the objects of your worship, I also found an altar with this inscription, "TO AN UNKNOWN GOD." What, therefore, you worship in ignorance, this I proclaim to you' (Acts 17:22–23). Paul, after finding a point they agreed upon, goes on to give a very clear summary of the Gospel adapted to their understanding. 'Now when they heard of the resurrection of the dead, some began to sneer, but others said, 'We shall hear you again concerning this' . . . but some men joined him and believed . . .' (Acts 17:22–23). It is questionable if any of them would have believed had Paul started straight in by aggressively sharing the Gospel and showing little regard for those in his audience.

The writer of Hebrews uses the same method. He anchors the Christian message to Jewish religion because it is the background of those he is writing to. His aim is to show them the truth by respecting their beliefs, and not to alienate them by attacking.

The most important point of all is to be a servant. Take the route of humility. Avoid arrogance and putting ourself above those we are trying to reach. Christ has called us to be servants, to take the path of humility. I take that to mean we freely admit our sins and weaknesses. We are not to dominate people by the sheer power of our personality, or dazzle them by the cleverness of our words. A humble attitude has more impact in evangelism than anything else we can do.

Don't do the Convicting

God does not sanction, or require that *we* bring conviction of sin to those people we talk to about salvation. If we try to do this we have stepped over the line and taken upon us the job of the Holy Spirit. 'And He (the Holy Spirit), when He comes, will convict the world concerning sin, and righteousness and judgement' (John 16:8).

At times I have tried to be the 'Holy Spirit' to others

and have been totally frustrated. I have learned that in His own time and way, the Holy Spirit will do the convicting, regardless of how hard I, in my own strength, try to make it happen. We must always remember that in evangelism it is our job to sow the seed of the Gospel in a person's heart. It is the job of the Holy Spirit to cause that seed to take root and bring forth a harvest of conviction, repentance, and new life.

Don't Manipulate

It is easy to manipulate people, and we live in a world that subtly does it everyday. Advertising bombards us from all sides trying to create false needs that will cause us to rush out and buy the products advertised. In such a world of manipulation we must be very careful not to employ the same means in evangelism.

Jesus did not manipulate people. He did not try to back them into corners where they could do nothing but what He wanted them to do. Always He presented the truth in love and allowed people the latitude to act upon it as they saw fit. Many responded to His message, others chose not to. We must be careful to follow this example in our evangelism. Always remember that just as easily as you can manipulate a person into accepting the Gospel and giving their life to Jesus, someone else can manipulate them out of it. People must choose for themselves based on the truth and love – that is the only way evangelism will be effective and long-lasting.

Chapter Seven

A Word About Soul Winning

The term 'soul winning' is in popular use in Christianity today. In many ways it is a positive term, expressing our commitment as believers to make Christ known, but it can also be a negative term, if it stands for unbiblical practices and attitudes. If it gives the impression that it is our prerogative to win a person's soul, which can make us 'technique' oriented – we become dependent on diagrams and recited lines. If the recipients say 'yes' in the appropriate gap, they're 'saved', if they say 'no' the game is over and it's time to go on to another person.

I can remember, as a teenager, travelling back from outreaches. The teams would reunite and our conversation would run along these lines:

'How many did you get today?'

'Oh, I got eight.'

'That's good, but I got thirteen, five more than you!'

'Well, it was a slow day for me, I had trouble warming up, and wasted a lot of time talking to someone who was not really open.'

As much as I hate to admit it, we were talking about leading people to Christ. Each 'conversion' represented another notch on our Bible cover! We had entirely missed the point that people are not just objects to be won. We centred our attention on techniques that would get the highest number of affirmative responses, instead of ministering to a person's needs. The term soul-winning implies that people are merely souls to be won and not people to be loved and respected. To treat people as lost souls is to reduce them to the level of an object, thus denigrating their value as someone created in God's image.

Jesus and his disciples presented the Gospel in a variety of ways. The same approach is never recorded twice in the New Testament. Sometimes Jesus talked in parables, other times He asked direct questions. He sent his disciples out two by two, but instead of giving them a pat formula to recite, he told them to be witnesses to what they had seen. If this approach was sufficient for the disciples, it should also be enough for us.

Our witnessing must be to the truth. The person we are witnessing to is not the focus, we are not trying to 'get them'. Instead, the focus is Jesus. We are witnessing all he has done for us. That is all He requires of us, that as a faithful witness we witness to the truth of what we understand and have experienced. It then becomes the job of the Holy Spirit to take our witness and use it to draw the person to Jesus. It is his job and we cannot do it for him.

It can be advantageous to learn how to effectively share our faith. It can be helpful to gather our thoughts into a systematic framework as we witness to the truth of what we know and have experienced. However, we must be careful not to use questions or approaches to witnessing in an assembly line fashion on every person we meet. No one wants to feel they are the 23rd person to have 'Plan Five B' tried on them.

Techniques are nothing more than tools which are sometimes appropriate to draw people into conversation and should be used sparingly and wisely. We, and not our technique, are what witnesses to the truth. No matter how elaborate and well crafted our technique is, our life, as a living reflection of Jesus, is what will touch the hearts of men and women.

If we're asked a question and don't know the answer, what should we do? We should be honest with the person and tell them we don't know the answer! Honesty is necessary and has a powerful effect when it comes from the heart. We are not trying to dazzle people with our knowledge, we are trying to communicate Jesus's loves to them.

If a person asks honest questions, a lack of answers can be a barrier to the person making a commitment to Christ. If this is the case, then it needs to be answered. Write down the questions people ask, and go home and research the answer. Ask someone who knows more about it for their input. When we have the answer, arrange to meet with the person again to discuss it.

Become familiar with good Christian literature which answers the most commonly asked questions (see Chapter Eight), and carry it with you. Ask the person if they would read it and meet with you again at a later date to discuss it. You may lose some books giving them out this way, but it is worth it for the joy of bringing a non-Christian into a relationship with Christ, or helping a person find answers to their questions.

Chapter Eight

Successful Evangelism?

There is tremendous pressure to be 'someone' in our society, and in many respects, social status depends upon 'success'. It is not surprising, then, that the same criteria is often used to evaluate our progress in evangelism.

Successful evangelism, however, is not based on the number of converts we've made, the array of witnessing techniques we know, the length of time we can stand on a street corner handing out tracts, or what evangelism seminars we have attended. Some of these things may aid our evangelism, but they do not make us effective evangelists.

Successful evangelism is firmly rooted in our willingness to get personally involved in the lives of non-Christians with a view to being a faithful witness to Christ. If that life is shallow and ineffectual then our evangelism will be the same. To be an effective evangelist we must first spend time developing our relationship with the Lord. That is not to infer we shouldn't share our faith until we are mature Christians, we should. What it means is that our emphasis must be on the quality of our Christian life and not the words or techniques we use. Jesus demonstrated this. It was his quality of life, and not his words which drew people. Indeed, there are instances recorded where the crowds had little idea of what he was talking about! Yet, there was a quality in his life that attracted and challenged all who came into contact with him.

In the final analysis it is God and not man who measures effectiveness in evangelism, and His standard has different reference points than ours. He is not going to judge us on the number of converts we have made in the course of our life. He is more interested in how we have lived our life before others and the impact it has had on those around us. Yes, we must share the Gospel, Jesus has commanded us to do so, but we must never forget we are dealing with people and not just statistics. We must respect people, honour them, win their confidence, and, in doing so, earn the right to speak with them about the Lord. When we make this our priority, the words we speak will deeply touch a person's life.

Perhaps you are wanting to know where to begin in sharing your faith. If you are looking for some specific steps and helps, let me suggest the following principles:

1. Pray regularly for three of four friends who are not Christians. Pray for them by name. Ask God for ways to serve your friends. Ask Him for ideas on how you can get more involved in their lives. Perhaps it will mean having them into your home, or helping them at their work. Perhaps a gift or a book would be meaningful.
2. Establish social relationships with the people you are praying for. Build a friendship with them in sports or through activities they enjoy. Develop mutual interests. If you do not have such friends it's time to start developing them.
3. Respond to the 'felt' needs of your friends. What do they feel they need? Answers to questions? A job? Food to eat? Love and acceptance? Help with family problems? A sense of importance? Respond by getting involved.
4. Get to know their objections to Christianity and, if they

have them, misconceptions of the Gospel. Develop thoughtful answers. As we respond to people's questions, we can do so with the knowledge that as Christians we have much to learn from them as well. We should cultivate an attitude of open inquiry and honest searching for truth. God has deposited the knowledge of Himself in all religions and cultures, and although He has uniquely revealed Himself through the Lord Jesus, there is much for us to learn from all faiths, cultures, and political perspectives.

5. Invite your friends to activities and events with other Christians. We should be sensitive to what types of events they would be most comfortable attending. Hopefully, they can taste the reality of Christian fellowship and see the love of Christ as it is expressed between brothers and sisters in the Lord.

Exactly how and when people come to the Lord through our sharing the Gospel we may never know. Conversion is a process, and it is difficult to tell exactly what part each of us plays in drawing a person to Christ. Some of us may be working in fields that are 'ready for harvest', others of us are planting seeds amid the rocky ground. What is important is that each of us functions under the direction of the Lord of the Harvest. We must concentrate on pleasing him. Jesus said, 'If I be lifted up from the earth, I will draw all men to Myself' (John 12:32). Let us always lift up Jesus as the one worthy of allegiance.

Chapter Nine

The Six Most Commonly Asked Questions

The following is a brief outline of six most asked questions. This list is in no way intended to be exhaustive. It will, however, provide ideas as to how such questions can be handled, and I hope they will spur you on to further research.

People ask questions for different reasons, and while we should think through possible answers to their questions, we should also be careful to discern why they are asking questions. There are people who do not really want to know the answer to their questions and there are others who ask questions to test us, to see if we are open and if we think deeply about our world. Sadly, some people ask questions just as a way of stopping us from witnessing to them. They hope to confuse us and throw us off in a smoke screen of difficult questions. At the other end of the scale there are those who ask questions out of a genuine interest and hunger for truth. By discerning a person's motive for asking a question we can better deal with the underlying issues. It will also help us in knowing how much time and effort to put into our answer. If the person is not interested in what we believe, it is best not to argue or press information on them. By being gracious with a seemingly callous or dishonest person, there is always the chance for truth to be quickened in their hearts. In the end, it is God who knows men's motives, not us.

However we discern the situation, we must be careful not to leave the impression that Christianity is only for the weak minded or those who are prepared to leave their brains at the church door. Christianity is a reasoned and historically rooted faith that offers the only valid answers to the problems of today's world. We have good news for our world that needs to be shared thoughtfully and with great wisdom and sensitivity.

At the end of this booklet is a list of books which will help in further research of these questions. They are also books that are helpful to have on hand to give to non-Christians. Never underestimate the potential of leaving good Christian literature with a seeking friend.

What About all the Hypocrites in Christianity?

A person who says one thing and does another is a hypocrite. We all know Christians who, at one time or another, have not lived up to what they proclaim. The reality, though, is that there will be hypocrites, no matter what we choose to align ourselves to. Let's say, for example, that I decide to be a schoolteacher so that I can guide and be an example to children. However, we have all read newspaper accounts of schoolteachers caught molesting their pupils. What am I to do? Do I not become a teacher because of some teachers who have betrayed the trust put in them? Or, do I go ahead and become a teacher and determine that I will never betray the trust put in me? To use another example, perhaps I am a doctor and my whole motivation for being one is to help alleviate the suffering of others. In the medical profession I discover there are those doctors who do not give their patients adequate care or help alleviate their suffering. There are even doctors who are prepared to let their patients die simply because they cannot pay the treatment fees. Do I give up my practice in disgust and shame at my fellow practitioners? No. To do so would put me in the same category as them. I would be doing to my patients exactly what I found so shameful in my fellow doctors – not providing them with proper medical care.

Hypocrisy is not confined to Christianity, and while the above examples are hypothetical they can be replaced many times over by actual incidents. We cannot allow the poor judgement, inconsistencies and mistakes of others to deter us. If we do it will destroy the hopes and plans we have for our life. There is a difference between hypocrisy and immaturity. Christians are not perfect, but they are forgiven. We should not allow a person's failures and weaknesses to keep us from the truth. We cannot let the behaviour of other people ruin a relationship with God, our Father. We cannot afford for the inconsistent behaviour of others to dictate the decisions we make in life.

Further, if we are able to discern hypocrisy in a person then we are also able to discern right from wrong. If we can discern right from wrong then we are responsible for doing what is right. Another person's wrong can never be our excuse for doing wrong ourselves.

Is Jesus the Only Way to God?

There are so many religions and their offshoots in our world that it seems difficult to believe only one is right – that Jesus is the only way to God.

While many would like to lump all religions together as man's various pursuits of God, Christiantiy does not lend itself to such categorization. Jesus said 'I am the way, and the truth, and the life; no one comes to the father, but through me.' (John 14:6). When a religious leader makes such a claim, he cannot be just a good man. Good men do not make such claims.

Christianity is in one sense an exclusive religion and cannot co-exist as just another 'way' to God. Jesus Christ said he was the Only Begotten Son of God. Buddha, on the other hand, saw himself as a seeker of truth, Mohammed believed he was a prophet, and Confucius was a sage. None of them ever claimed to be God's only Son. If Jesus is right then He is the only way to God, and while other religions may contain certain elements of truth they can never of themselves lead us to a relationship with the Creator of the universe. All religions can be false, but they cannot all be true. When two religions make contradictory claims on the same point, they have to either be right or wrong. For example, Muslims claim that Judas, not Jesus, died on the cross. Both views cannot be correct.

If Jesus is the only way to God, then what about those who have never heard of him? The Bible says that Jesus was 'the true light which, coming into the world, enlighten every man' (John 1:9). I believe that within every tribe and people group, God has placed elements of truth that, if followed, will lead a person to God (Romans 1:19 – 20, 2:12 – 16). I also believe that those who seek the truth will readily embrace the Gospel message when it is presented to them. Not all people have the opportunity to hear the Gospel, but if they have lived according to the truth God has revealed to them, then God will judge them fairly. One thing is certain, people are not sent to hell for rejecting a Jesus they have never heard of. Men go to hell because they reject the truth – the truth they know. Men cannot come to God without forgiveness through Jesus Christ, but they certainly are not judged for something they do not know. In one sense, there are many ways to God, but they all lead to one way. Let me explain this truth in the following way: if religion is man's way to search for God, then Jesus is God's way to search for man. Someone once said religions are like many roads that lead to the top of the mountain. If that is true, I believe Jesus stands at the top of that mountain! He is the way God has provided for man's forgiveness. No other religion provides for that.

If Jesus is who He claims to be, and who the Bible says He is, He is unique. That results in an exclusiveness, but not out of pride or paternalism. If God sent His Son into the world, and God has chosen to use the death of His Son as the way to forgive man for his sins, then Jesus is indeed the only way to God. That does not mean there is no truth in other religions, but truth is only truth as long as it is consistent with God's revelation of Himself through His Son, the Lord Jesus, and with the revelaton of faith of truth in the Bible.

Was Jesus a Religious Leader?

This question is closely related to the one above. Anyone who is seriously seeking to know the truth about God must decide who exactly Jesus was. There are four conclusions we can come to about who Jesus was. He was either: a liar, a lunatic, a legend, or who he claimed to be – the Son of God. Let's look at these four possibilities.

A) He was a liar
Jesus made many claims about himself. He claimed to be the Son of God who would go before us to prepare a place in heaven. He also claimed to be the Way, the Truth, and the Life. If Jesus knew this to be concocted nonsense when he said it, he was a liar and a hypocrite on a grand scale. His lies have inspired more men and women to change the way they live more than any other event in history, and if what he promises is not true, then to raise the hopes and expectations of so many people falsely makes Him a fraud and not a great man.

Jesus was consistent in all aspects of His life. He never gave foolish answers, His life was a living reflection of the things He spoke about, and He never reneged on a stand He had taken, even when He knew it would lead to His crucifixion. It is strange that a man whose actions were very consistent in the face of difficulties could have had one monstrous inconsistency – lying.

Before his crucifixion Jesus had ample opportunity to back down, but He did not. Even while dying on the cross He held firm to all He had said. Why? To gain a following, or prestige? As a result of His deliberate choices, He had neither prestige nor a following at the time of his death. His disciples had denied Him, and His own people, the Jews, ridiculed Him. If Jesus lied to gain personal gratification, then He certainly did not receive what He sought.

B) He was a lunatic

'The historical difficulty of giving for the life, saying and influence of Jesus any explanation that is not harder than the Christian explanation is very great. The discrepancy between the depth and the sanity of His moral teaching and the rampant megalomania which must life behind His theological teachings unless He is indeed God has never been satisfactorily explained,' C.S. Lewis (Miracles, A Preliminary Study. Macmillan).

Lewis's point is a sound one. How could a man so deceived about himself and his mission consistently prove, in every respect, to others that he was worth living and dying for? Of the 12 disciples, one killed himself when faced with the realization he had betrayed the Son of God, the other 11 dedicated their lives to preaching the Gospel, and ten of them were killed in the course of doing that. If Jesus were a lunatic it seems inconceivable that He could have elicited such dedication from His followers.

C) He was a legend

The writers of the Gospels were convinced Jesus existed. They recorded his birthplace and genealogy, and told us where He lived and worked and when and how He died. He is linked to prominent religious and political leaders who would have denied His existence had they never met Him. There is nothing vague or ethereal about these facts – they were written with sincerity and intended to pass the scrutiny of all who read them.

No serious historian denies the existence of Christ. The idea that Jesus never lived holds no validity for the student of history as there is simply too much evidence to the contrary. Independent of Christian writings Jesus is noted in contemporary Roman and Jewish historical records. Indeed, it is no more complex to prove the existence of Jesus Christ as an historical figure than it is to prove the existence of Julius Caesar.

D) He was the Son of God

Jesus asked Peter, 'Who do you think I am?' Each of us must answer that question for ourselves. If Jesus is not a liar, lunatic or legend we are left with only one alternative – He was the Son of God. He was not a good man or a great prophet for, in fact, one cannot at the same time be God and a mere prophet or great religious leader.

Many people do not want to reach that conclusion. They many give tacit mental assent to the notion, but are unwilling to go any further since being convinced that Jesus really is the Son of God involves making moral choices that will affect their lives forever.

Why Does a Good God Send People to Hell?

The blame for sending people to hell does not lie with God, but with those who wilfully and deliberately reject a loving

Saviour in favour of pursuing their own ends and desires. There are consequences to our actions both in this life and in the life to come. If a person decides they have no need of God in this life, why should they be forced to live in His eternal presence in the next life? God does not want anybody to perish and face an eternity in hell, but many people choose to. Before you react too strongly to this idea of eternity in hell, let's consider the following truths the Bible teaches about heaven and hell.

Heaven and hell are extensions of how people have chosen to live their life on earth. Heaven is freedom from the restrictions of our earthly body and being able to know God more completely. Heaven is a quality of life that begins now: 'This is eternal life, to know Thee, the only true God, and Jesus Christ whom Thou has sent' (John 17:3). Hell is an endless life of complete selfishness that can never be gratified. Many people don't have to wait until they die to be in hell, they are already there, trapped in a maze of guilt, fear, and frustration because of the choices they have made thus far in life.

Recently, a friend shared with me how he had to nurse his grandmother as she was dying. As the grandmother approached death the things she'd done in life came back to haunt her. In her case, she had chosen to have several abortions. As she lay in her bed, the choices she'd made so many years before began tormenting her. She would sit straight up and let out blood-curdling screams then curl up and weep for the children she had aborted. 'She didn't need to die to be in hell, she was there already,' my friend relayed. How tragic this is, yet without Christ people are prisoners to the wrong choices they have made in life and, in a sense, are already living in hell. To me, forcing men to spend eternity in the presence of a holy God they do not want to serve would be a greater hell itself.

When the Bible uses fire to describe hell, I agree with Billy Graham that it is symbolic of the intense torment eternal separation from God is. It is an attempt by the writers of the Bible to capture the awesome terribleness of eternity without God.

' "As I live!" declares the Lord God, "I take no pleasure in the death of the wicked, but rather that the wicked turn from his way and live. Turn back, turn back from your evil ways! Why then will you die?" ' (Ezekiel 33:11).

Why do the Innocent Suffer?

Seeing a starving child die in it's mother's arms; reading of a mass shooting of customers as they sat eating their dinner in a restaurant, or visiting a leukaemia ward in a hospital and gazing into the faces of children who have no hope of recovery, tears at the heart. Something deep inside tells us this is not right, these are innocent victims and there ought not to be this kind of suffering in the world.

Why does a loving God allow such things to happen? If He is willing to stop the innocent from suffering but lacks the power to do so, then He is not the all-powerful God He claims to be. However, if He does not want the innocent to suffer and has the ability to stop it, we are faced with a dilemma – why do the innocent continue to suffer?

First, I must point out that the word 'suffering' loses its meaning if there is no God. If all of life is reduced to physical and chemical laws, what is man but a highly developed group of cells and matter? Matter in itself has no lasting or spiritual value if we are mere accidents, a result of the fortuitous coming together of matter many millions of years ago. Suffering implies spiritual values, a soul and a conscience.

Suffering cannot be 'wrong' if there are no moral absolutes. Wrong means it should not happen. If there is no God there are no moral absolutes, and without God's laws nothing is 'morally' wrong. For the 'innocent' to suffer, there must be guilt, and real guilt comes from violating moral absolutes.

The very fact that we are repulsed by suffering is an indication that God exists, however difficult we find the presence of suffering in this world. One cannot simply deny the existence of God as a way of handling this terrible problem.

I don't know *any* easy answers to this question, from Christians or non-Christians. I do know that this world is not the way God created it. It is fallen. Man has turned against God, and since that has happened the creation has been marked by alienation. Let us say that suffering is wrong, but let us not just discuss this as a philosophical or religious problem. Let us weep over our world. Jesus did. When He stood before the tomb of His friend, Lazarus, Jesus was angry. He was hurt by death and its accompanying pain. But he also acted. He raised Lazarus from the dead, as if to say to all mankind that death is not final. There is an answer though we do not fully comprehend why He allows this world to keep going, we can look forward to His redemption. Some day, He will redeem all creation. Though I don't fully understand God, I trust Him. What I know of Him gives me reason to trust. Some day I will stand before Him and then I will ask some questions.

Not to believe in God gives *far more* questions than if we do believe in Him. Atheism is no answer to the problem of suffering. It only lessens the meaning of one's suffering, implying that life is all chance and has no spiritual meaning or eternal reality. Life is more than a cosmic game. There are morally guilty and morally innocent people. They both suffer; I wish it on no man, especially the innocent child and defenceless mother, but I refuse to blame God for all of this. I have helped make this fallen world what it is. I struggle with pride, anger, lust, greed, and all the other sins of mankind that have destroyed God's world. No, God is not at fault. He came into this fallen world, and though He was one with us, He never sinned. He did not remain aloof in heaven; He came to us, he died and He rose again. He pointed the way to the future. He conquered death and sin and He promised that He would return to end all suffering. That is our hope.

God did not create man to suffer, but He did create man with a free will. Man can choose to suffer and/or inflict his suffering on others. To say we should not be able to affect each other in a negative way is to take away our freedom of choice. Every time a negative act was committed God would have to intervene and disallow it. In so doing He would override our right to make free choices. In such a world, good acts would lose their significance since they would be the only kind of acts permissible.

The innocent ought not to suffer – yes – and God has inscribed that along with a sense of justice on each of our hearts. God has also prepared a place for us where there will be no suffering. 'Behold, the dwelling of God is with men. He will dwell with them, and they shall his people, and God himself will be with them; he will wipe away every tear from their eyes, and death shall be no more, neither shall there be mourning nor crying nor pain any more, for the former things have passed away' (Revelation 21:3 – 4). Presently, however, the innocent do suffer, not because of the impotence of a loving and all-powerful God, but because of the wilful choices of people who choose to impinge upon the lives of other people and, in so doing, cause heart-wrenching suffering in our world.

Why are Christians not Concerned with Social Injustice?

At present there is a political climate that has elicited a strong movement amongst Bible-believing Christians in the United States to identify with conservative and right-wing political figures and movements. The agenda of these groups is normally concerned with abortion, the family education, pornography, and defence. The influence of this movement is international in nature, so Christians of all nations are influenced by it. Because American T.V. evangelists are spokesmen for this movement and have powerful influence through the media, the non-Christian press has given much attention to Jim Bakker, Jerry Falwell, Jimmy Swaggart and Pat Robertson, and their personal lives and political views. Simultaneously, international attention has been focused on disarmament, refugees, poverty, unemployment, urban decay, and political tyranny from both right and left. With many politicians dealing with these issues, and the political right identified with another agenda, the impression has grown in the minds of many people that 'born-again' Christians either are not concerned with broader issues of social political realities, or, if they are, they seem to consistently defend the status quo. Rarely do conservative Christians speak for peace, greater opportunities for the poor, human rights, better working conditions and *against* injustice, oppression, and political tyranny on the right. This has given many socially aware non-Christians the impression that Biblical Christians have no concern for social justice and that therefore the Bible has nothing to say about the issues. If a person rejects the Gospel because they are concerned for the poor and the oppressed, and they have the idea that Christianity has nothing to say about these issues, then our evangelism must involve giving witness to what God's Word has to say about these important matters. We cannot be silent on any issue that the Bible teaches about clearly.

God is against economic injustice as well as pornography; He is for peace as well as godly education; the Lord opposes abortion; He is pro-life, pro-family, and pro-human rights; our Father in heaven hates pride, lust, greed, violence, and political corruption. He warns the rich man and the lazy man alike. He is against idolatry, immorality, and exploitation of the weak and defenceless. If we have a selective indignation against some kinds of evil but not others, we not only appear to be partial to sin, we are. We must oppose sin in our own lives and collective sin in society that results in large numbers of people being hurt, exploited and used. Sin always works through people and against people. God speaks for the sinned against, and offers mercy to the repentant sinner.

Developing a Biblical awareness and sensitivity to the corporate nature of evil and the cultural bondages that wound and damage people is an important part of our witness as Biblical Christians. Many non-Christians are deeply, deeply concerned about the hundreds of millions of people in our world who are suffering. We who are Christians have much to learn from those with a sensitive social conscience. Not to do so is arrogant and leaves our witness to the Lord Jesus incomplete and innocuous.

There are six questions or issues often raised by non-Christians. As we ask God for His help, He will give us wisdom and the power of the Holy Spirit to be his witnesses.

Dear Lord Jesus,
I confess my need to have more boldness, more wisdom, and more faithfulness as a witness to your love and truth. Anoint me with your Spirit and stir my heart to be faithful to you and available to share your Good News with my non-Christian family, friends, and neighbours.

In Jesus Name,

Amen

Chapter Ten

The Power of the Page

Perhaps no other form of evangelism can appear to be so impersonal as that of handing a tract to someone, especially a perfect stranger. If you had been asked, before you were a Christian, if a printed tract could be effective in communicating the Gospel, most likely you would have thought of an experience where you were offended by somebody pushing literature under your nose and instantly said, 'Of course not!'

Most of us assume that the printed page is too impersonal and too impotent to affect the kind of life-changing decision demanded by the Gospel.

How can anyone not already attuned to God encounter the living Christ through a 'religious' looking piece of paper? Yet thousands and thousands of people regularly find Jesus Christ through the printed page. I have been amazed time and again to see people coming to the Lord Jesus Christ as a direct result of reading a moving testimony in a book, God's Word, or a well-written tract. I heard recently of a member of a well-known motorcycle bike gang coming to know the Lord by reading a gospel of John. A friend of mine was handed a tract on a street as a young tourist in Germany. After reading it alone in her hotel room, she prayed and accepted Christ as her Saviour. One of our young evangelists in Amsterdam had his appetite whetted for the Gospel by reading a pictorial book about Jerusalem in a friend's home in Sweden years ago. Even though he was smoking hashish, something touched his heart deeply as he thought about the Jesus of Palestine. Several months later he accepted Jesus as his personal Saviour and Lord.

Recently, a Buddhist monk in Burma, became curious about what the Christians believed, and decided to read the entire Bible through non-stop. After doing so he accepted Christ into his life. He did this before he had met a single Christian.

On the face of it, 'literature evangelism' seems like a contradiction in terms, especially to those of us who are very relational in our orientation. But it is important to remember that many people appreciate the opportunity to have time alone with a piece of literature so that they can reflect and think about whether or not they will become a Christian. There are some people who are more responsive to the Gospel once they have time to think it over in the privacy of their home rather than confrontation with another person.

When people read the truth of the gospel, even if a particular chapter and verse in the Bible is not referred to, it is still God's truth. The Bible says that 'the Gospel is the power of God unto salvation' (Romans 1:16).

There are certain advantages to 'literature evangelism'. The printed page is easily and inexpensively transmitted to very large numbers of people. With a small budget and simple technology, one can easily reach hundreds or thousands, perhaps millions, of people in a very straightforward manner.

The printed page is permanent – it does not fade away like a radio or television programme. It can stay on the shelf or sit on the corner coffee table. It can be carried home with you in a pocket. It can be read in private, and then it can be read again. It can be scanned quickly or read slowly; it can be studied again and again by the interested person, whether riding on a bus, squatting on a street corner, or sitting on an aeroplane.

Unlike other forms of media, the printed page communicates in a form which is retainable for visually oriented people. Literature is particularly suitable for some non-Western cultures where a strong dependence on television has not taken place. Many people in the non-Western world do not take the printed page for granted. There is a thirst for learning and a quest for knowledge. In simple openness, many people will take what is written at face value. They esteem printed words and give them great respect.

David Stravers, in an article entitled *Print Power: An Incarnational Approach to Literature Evangelism in Cities* (Urban Missions, Volume Five, number 5), says there need not be a divorce between personalness and effective communication through literature.

There are two principles stressed by Stravers' writing that I think should help make this point:

1: Literature Evangelism should be person-centred, not just message-centred.

The person we are giving the literature to should be the focus of our communication, not just the message we want to communicate. Good communication is not merely the transfer of certain facts from someone who has it to someone who does not.

We must be careful to give literature prayerfully and with much consideration as to what tract or book would be appropriate for the particular person we are giving it to. Does it fit their spiritual situation? Is it dealing with questions they are asking? Is it appropriate to their personality and thinking processes?

Literature evangelism is defined as: giving a tract, booklet, Gospel portion, or book in an attempt to communicte the Gospel to another person. At the heart of the Gospel is relationship, therefore, every piece of literature given should be done in such a manner that it is not offensive to the person receiving it. In some cultures, you can hand out large portions of scripture and people will remain interested and very few pieces will be discarded. In other cultures, indiscriminate distribution of literature can be either offensive, or greatly lessen the value of that which is handed out. It is this personal approach that makes our literature evangelism sensitive to the person we are giving it to.

2: Effective Literature Evangelism Involves Dialogue and Reciprocity

Not only should a piece of literature be handed to a person, but there should be a way of following through. If it is a book given to a friend, I think we should discuss it with them later. What did they think of it? What were their objections? What were their questions? This personal interaction is a vital step in the relational aspect of literature evangelism. When people do respond to the literature that is given to them, there must be some means of follow-through. Perhaps a correspondence course offered at the end of the piece of the literature, a telephone number they can call, or a meeting or service they can attend. Though there may not be large numbers of people responding immediately, there must be *some* way they can respond.

I have often given a piece of literature in response to receiving one. I have committed myself to read, as an exchange of ideas, many books and tracts both from non-Christian friends and members of religious cults.

I do this in faith that God's truth will triumph over anything else. I believe that as a mature and stable Christian, it will not hurt me to be open to other's views and ideas and that this will be vitally important in an ongoing dialogue in the relationship with people that I am seeking to win to Christ. Not only is it important to do this in order to communicate my openness as a Christian (sadly, many Christians give the impression that they have closed their minds to learning by their unwillingness to read or consider what other people have found important), but it also provides vital and personal communication with non-Christians.

Prayer over the literature is like watering a seed placed in dry ground. It gives opportunity for growth. Prayer also protects the seed so it is not carried away by the wind or by wild birds. It is through prayer that God can also direct us to the right piece of literature for the right person.

Never underestimate the power of the printed page. God's truth can touch people's hearts in many ways. Christian books have been placed in the hands of French philosophers, Kings and Queens, business moguls, terrorists, and quiet peasant workers. He has promised to send His spirit wherever His truth is proclaimed.

Keep alert, perhaps today you can send a printed missionary on a quiet journey, waiting patiently for its opportunity to find a way into the enquiring mind and searching heart of its reader.

Chapter Eleven

Overcoming Fear

I once heard a man say 'To love lost souls to me is no chore, my big problem is the man next door.'

It certainly is no chore to love people who don't know Christ and live a thousand miles away. It is much easier to do that than to speak up to our school mate, the person who works with us in the office, or our neighbour who is obnoxious and critical.

When it is time to speak up to a person, to lovingly confront them with the Christ's claim to rule over their life, there is that sinking feeling in the pit of the stomach, that worry about what they will think, a feeling of insecurity and uncertainty about what words we will use. Thoughts flow quickly. 'What will they think? Will they mock me? Will they just think I am a fool?

Proverbs 29:25 warns, 'The fear of man brings a snare.' At one time or another, Billy Graham, and every other Christian, has experienced fear when it comes to personally sharing the Gospel.

I know I have. I remember a situation that illustrates this. I was 19 years of age and I was going from door-to-door to share the gospel for the first time in my life. I went up to the first door and knocked. When the lady of the house came in, I said very nervously, 'Hello, this is my friend, John, my name is Jesus Christ and we would like to talk to you about . . .' I was so nervous that I introduced myself as Jesus!

Fortunately, the humour of the moment broke the ice and the lady asked what these two teenagers at her door really wanted to talk about. I confessed my nervousness and then told her our purpose was simply to tell people about the joy and forgiveness we had found in Christ. Much to my amazement, she stood in the door and listened for quite some time. She was deeply touched by the simple testimony we gave of our personal relationship with Christ.

Different Kinds of Fear

It might be helpful to examine more carefully the kinds of fear that people experience and why these fears keep people from sharing their faith in Jesus Christ. Danny Lehman in his book *Bringing 'Em Back Alive*, mentions several different kinds of fear.

The first is the fear of rejection. This is particularly true in our performance-oriented Western world. If we wear the right clothes, say the right things, wear the right cologne, then we will be accepted. We are raised from our earliest moments to be accepted by others. There is a deep fear that people will reject us or think we are crazy if we say the wrong thing or act a bit foolish.

It is helpful to remember that Jesus was 'despised and rejected of men' (Isaiah 53:3). There are times when people will reject us because of what we share with them. Perhaps it will be out of misunderstanding, or maybe because the Holy Spirit is convicting them of their own sin.

Most people go through a stage where they become very angry and bitter toward Christians because of a deep awareness of their own sinfulness. We must be willing to bear this rejection, and to lovingly and graciously continue to be faithful, to share the gospel of Jesus Christ. If we allow fear of rejection to keep us from speaking up, many who desperately need Christ, and secretely in their hearts want peace and forgiveness, will not find Him.

Danny Lehman points out in his book that the Bible assures us that 'in the fear of the Lord there is strong confidence and his children shall have refuge' (Proverbs 14:26). If we put our trust in the Lord, He will give us confidence. He will take the most shy, timid person and give them the quiet assurance so that they can speak boldly and forcefully of what they believe.

People speak openly about their sexual exploits, their political convictions, their views about philosophy, the weather, sports, and every other thing else that enters their minds. Why is it that we as Christians do not have the right to share our convictions?

I am not talking about forcing something on other people. There is a difference between experiencing rejection because of the way we say something and the message we share. If someone rejects us because we are belligerent or insensitive then that is our responsibility. But if we simply share our beliefs about God, man, or the nature of sin and people reject us, then that shows a lack of depth and tolerance on their part. That is their problem, not ours. We must not allow the unwillingness to listen openingly to what we have to say keep us from sharing our faith.

I challenge you now, and I do it as one who has often failed in this area, to choose to obey the Lord and to use every opportunity possible to speak up regardless of the possibility of rejection.

Fear of losing our reputation is the second kind of fear. As Danny Lehman points out in his book, the best way to deal with the fear of losing our reputation is to give up our reputation! We are to follow the example of the Lord Jesus. Paul mentions the fact that Jesus gave up His own reputation (Philippians 2:7).

We must be more concerned about what God thinks of

us than what people think. In fact, the big question in life is not, 'Can we trust God?' but 'Can God trust us?' Will we be faithful and loyal to Him in every situation.

There comes a point when we must recognize that these inner-fears that we experience can produce sin. If we allow our fear to determine our actions, then we have become a slave to our fears. The Bible says the primary way to deal with fear, as with all sin, is through confession. John 1:9 says, 'If we confess our sins, he is faithful and just to forgive us and to cleanse us from all unrighteousness.'

A third kind of fear is the fear of physical harm. I have experienced this walking through the inner-city of Amsterdam. Some of our evangelists in Youth with a Mission have spoken of the fear of people retaliating against them physically.

I have had threats against my life so this is very personal and real to me. I have had to come to the place where I can honestly say to the Lord, 'I don't like pain and I don't want to die. I feel that if I face a situation where my life is threatened, I might deny you. But Lord, I trust you. I believe you are able to give me the grace I need when I face that kind of a situation. Therefore, I choose to trust that you are able to help me in any situation I face.'

The best way to overcome the fear of physical harm is to acknowledge it, confess it, and affirm our trust in the Lord. He is able to give us the grace to face any situation, *when* we face it. Don't live in such fear of anticipated danger that you miss the joy of God's love right now.

The fourth fear is that of being inadequate. This is the kind of fear that makes us afraid that we will not have the right words to say when we talk to someone, or they will ask us a question that we will not be able to answer. This is the simplest kind of fear and the easiest to overcome. It is through reading books on evangelism (some are listed in the Suggested Further Reading at the back of this book) that helps us to overcome this fear. I also encourage you to attend courses, schools, and classes on this subject. If you had an inadequacy and you had to overcome it to do the job, then you would most likely enrol in a training course offered for your work. In other words, people take practical steps to get the tools they need in order to do the job they have to do. It is the same way with evangelism. God can give us the tools we need to do the job. If we will seek Him and practically reach out and equip ourselves, then soon our fear will leave.

In fact, as we get experience, we begin to learn that most questions fall into a pattern (see Chapter Eight for the questions most often faced in evangelism). We can learn to anticipate them and how to answer them. People's objections to Christianity are often pretty superficial. It will not take you long, through some practical experience, to learn how to deal with them. Besides that, what most people want to hear is your personal testimony. They are impressed with joy, peace, and a sense of reality in a person's life. That is the one thing that you have that no one can deny!

Christians in the early church also faced these kinds of fear. Look at the situation in chapter four in the book of Acts and how those Christians responded to it: 'And now, Lord, take note of their threats and grant that thy bondservants may speak thy word with all confidence . . . and when they had prayed . . . they were all filled with the Holy Spirit and began to speak the word of God with boldness (Acts 4:29–31).

God is able to deliver us from all fears. In fact, the Bible says that 'perfect love casts out all fear.' One of the greatest ways to overcome fear is by choosing to pray for people and to love them with God's love. A practical way to do this is to take the names of three non-Christians and begin to pray for them on a regular basis. Ask the Lord to give you thoughts on how to pray for them and how to love them in a practical manner. Pray that they will have understanding of the Gospel. Pray that God will lead them to Christian friends who they will be able to listen to. Pray that they will be able to find literature that will speak to them about their needs for God. Pray that they will hear the Gospel through the media. Pray that they will come to a place physically and emotionally where they will cry out to God in their hearts. These are just some of the ways we can pray.

Receive God's love for these individuals by faith. It is an act of faith, not feeling to love people, especially when they are difficult to love. Ask God to fill your heart with His love for them. He will gladly do it. People will begin to see the difference in you. You can also ask God to give you inspiration and thoughts about how you can express that love to people in a practical way.

Perfect love, God's love, does drive out our fear. If we stop thinking about ourselves and we start thinking about others, effective evangelism will begin!

Suggested further reading:

Evidence That Demands a Verdict; More Evidence That Demands a Verdict, Josh McDowell. (Campus Crusade for Christ International.)
Mere Christianity, C.S. Lewis.
The Problem of Pain, C.S. Lewis.
Miracles, A Preliminary Study, C.S. Lewis. (Macmillan)
The Father Heart of God, Floyd McClung, Jr.
Living on the Devil's Doorstep, Floyd McClung, Jr.
Eternity in Their Hearts; Peace Child, Don Richardson.
I Dared to Call Him Father, B. Sheikh. (Revell)
Out of the Salt Shaker, Rebecca Pippert.
Bringing 'em Back Alive, Danny Lehman.
Everyday Evangelism, Billy Heuks, Jr.

Other Marshall Pickering Paperbacks

RICH IN FAITH

Colin Whittaker

Colin Whittaker's persuasive new book is written for ordinary people all of whom have access to faith, a source of pure gold even when miracles and healing seem to happen to other people only.

The author identifies ten specific ways to keep going on the road to faith-riches, starting where faith must always begin—with God himself, the Holy Spirit, the Bible, signs and wonders, evangelism, tongues and finally to eternal life with Christ.

OUR GOD IS GOOD

Yonggi Cho

This new book from Pastor Cho describes the blessings, spiritual and material, that reward the believer. Yonggi Cho presents his understanding of the fullness of salvation, bringing wholeness to God's people.

HEARTS AFLAME
Stories from the Church of Chile

Barbara Bazley

Hearts Aflame is a book suffused with love for the large, sometimes violent country of Chile and joy at the power of the Gospel taking root.

Each chapter is a story in itself, telling of some encounter, episode of friendship that has left its mark on the author's life.

If you wish to receive *regular information* about *new books*, please send your name and address to:

Name..

Address ....

....

....

....

I am especially interested in:

☐ Biographies
☐ Fiction
☐ Christian living
☐ Issue related books
☐ Academic books
☐ Bible study aids
☐ Children's books
☐ Music
☐ Other subjects